Epidemics

ANN KRAMER

FRANKLIN WATTS
LONDON•SYDNEY

First published in 2006 by Franklin Watts
338 Euston Road, London NW1 3BH

Franklin Watts Australia
Hachette Children's Books
Level 17/207 Kent Street
Sydney NSW 2000

Editor: Adrian Cole
Series design: White Design
Picture research: Diana Morris

A CIP catalogue record for this book is available from the British Library.

ISBN-10: 0-7496-6929-2
ISBN-13: 978-0-7496-6929-4

Dewey Classification: 614.4

Acknowledgements:
Action Press/Rex Features: 20. AP/Empics: 9, 26. Biblioteca Nacional Madrid/Dagli Orti/
Art Archive: 8b. Jack Clark/Image Works/Topfoto: 22. Saurabh Das/Empics: 27. Jim Dowdalls/
Science Photo Library: 18t. Fotomas/Topfoto: 8t. Boris Grdanoski/AP Empics: 14.Victor Habbick
Visions/Science Photo Library: 11. Peter Hvizdak/Image Works/Topfoto: 10. Sung Yeon-
Jae/AP/Empics: 19. Martin Keene/Empics: 29. Keystone/Topfoto: 5, 21b. Bill Lai/Image
Works/Topfoto: 18b. Yves Logghe/AP/Empics: 4. Richard Lord/Image Works/Topfoto: 25.
Samir Mizban/AP/Empics: 23. Photri/Topfoto: 24. Picturepoint/Topham: 6. Philippe Psaila/Science
Photo Library: 15. Sipa Press/Rex Features: front cover. Sean Sprague/Image Works/Topfoto: 16.
Sygma/Corbis: 21t. Syracuse Newspapers/Image Works/Topfoto: 17. Tatan Syuflana/AP/Empics:13.
Vincent Thian/AP/Empics: 12. Topfoto: 7. Chris Ware/Image Works/Topfoto: 28.

Every attempt has been made to clear copyright. Should there be any
inadvertent omission please apply to the publisher for rectification.

Printed in China

Franklin Watts is a division of Hachette Children's Books.

CONTENTS

EPIDEMICS IN THE NEWS

HOW DO YOU FEEL when you hear that a new and possibly deadly epidemic has broken out? What does the word 'epidemic' mean to you? Is it a deadly plague that may kill thousands of people a very long way away? Or do you think it is something that could affect you?

⬇ *A press conference in Brussels, Belgium, held after health officials announced a patient had been admitted to hospital with symptoms of bird flu (see pages 12–13). Tests later revealed the patient did not have the virus.*

NEWS COVERAGE

When it comes to disease, media coverage can be scary. Maybe you have read dramatic reports about a new 'superbug' in hospitals called MRSA, which kills patients. Or you have heard about so-called bird flu, which some experts predict could have a devastating impact on our lives? News headlines scream about killer bugs and life-threatening diseases.

NEW DISEASES

Sometimes watching the news makes it seem as though a whole range of new and deadly diseases are threatening our lives. How true is this? According to the World Health Organization (WHO) about 30 deadly infectious diseases have appeared since 1980. They include HIV/Aids, Ebola, SARS and legionnnaire's disease.

↑ *The Tamiflu drug is used to fight the human form of bird flu. Production of Tamiflu doubled in 2006 to anticipate an increase in demand.*

CROSSING BORDERS

Sometimes the movement of a disease takes the scientific community by surprise. In 1999, for example, doctors were startled when people near New York City, USA developed West Nile fever, a highly infectious disease formerly only known in Africa (see page 22).

NEWS TRENDS

Media coverage of disease outbreaks can be patchy. When they first occur the story often makes the news headlines, but coverage fades away, especially if the threat is in a far away country. Sometimes headlines are only made when a new disease hits countries in the developed world. HIV/Aids was headline news in the 1980s. Now it rarely gets a mention, even though it remains the most devastating epidemic of modern times, and is killing a whole generation of people in Africa.

WHAT DO YOU THINK?

According to some medical experts, the world has become much more vulnerable to the widespread threat of both new and old infectious diseases.

● What do you think about diseases and epidemics?

● Do you think the media makes the dangers seem worse than they are? Why would they want to?

● Why do you think newspapers make their news coverage of diseases so dramatic?

● Why might epidemics only make news when they break out in developed countries?

WHAT IS AN EPIDEMIC?

EPIDEMICS ARE *diseases, such as flu, measles or malaria that pass quickly from person to person. Sometimes a disease only infects a few people. When a lot of people become ill at the same time, it becomes an epidemic. An epidemic may last weeks, months, or even years.*

ENDEMIC AND PANDEMIC

If an infectious disease occurs regularly in one place it is described as endemic. For example, West Nile fever was once considered endemic to Africa. If an infectious disease spreads across the world, it is described as pandemic. HIV/Aids is a modern pandemic: it now exists on every continent.

GETTING ILL

We can catch infectious diseases in many ways: through physical touch, picking up germs from surfaces, sexual contact or breathing in germ-filled droplets that someone else has coughed or sneezed into the air. Insects, such as mosquitoes and ticks, carry disease-causing organisms and parasites. They spread them by biting us or infecting the food we eat and the water we drink. Sometimes we can catch diseases from close contact with animals, such as birds or pigs.

⬇ Cities, buses and trains crowded with people are perfect for helping to spread infectious diseases. Flu germs, for example, pass easily from one person to another in a cough or sneeze.

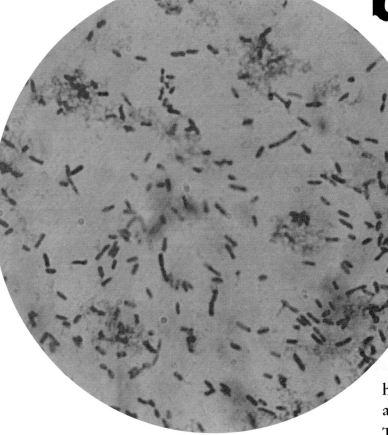

↑ *This is* bacterium dysenteriae *as seen under a microscope (magnified 1,000 times). It causes diarrhoea in humans.*

Germs – tiny microscopic organisms – cause infectious diseases by invading and attacking the human body. Viruses and bacteria are the most common types.

● A virus is a tiny package of chemicals. It breaks into living cells, including human cells. Once inside, it takes over the cell's chemical processes so the cell no longer works properly. Instead it just reproduces the virus.

● Bacteria are the smallest of living things. They are all around us – in the air, and on plants and animals – they even live inside us. Many are harmless, but some cause diseases such as cholera and tuberculosis (TB).

The human body fights disease by producing antibodies that attack invading organisms. If the body survives, it develops immunity against that specific disease.

ENCOURAGING DISEASE

Infectious diseases cause hundreds of thousands of deaths across the world each year. Some environmental experts say we are making matters worse. Increasing global travel, pollution and damage to the environment are helping to spread disease and encourage new illnesses. According to WHO, about 25 per cent of new diseases are the result of environmental damage, such as cutting down the rainforests. As trees are felled, animals and insects lose their natural habitats and some die. Bacteria-carrying parasites move to find new hosts – us.

COSTS OF DISEASE

Epidemics can kill many people, but they also affect social and economic life. For example, fear can discourage tourists from travelling to a region suffering from an epidemic. Local people cannot find work, so the economy suffers. An epidemic also puts a great strain on health services. Malaria and HIV/Aids are part of the reason many African countries still suffer from poverty. Money is diverted to providing medicine and staff to treat people who are ill. Even in developed countries an epidemic could stretch health services because of the rush for medical treatment.

EPIDEMICS HAVE *occurred throughout history – they are not new. They first started when humans settled in communities and began living close to animals, which passed on diseases. The number of epidemics increased as people began travelling and trading over greater distances. The growth of cities also encouraged epidemics.*

EARLY EPIDEMICS

One of the earliest epidemics occurred in Ancient Greece in 430 BCE. It was one of several events that led to the collapse of the great civilization of Athens around 338 BCE. Then, during the 1300s, a devastating epidemic called bubonic plague swept across Asia and Europe. It became known as the Black Death and was passed on by rat fleas carried on ships – although no one knew this at the time. There was no cure and millions of people died.

MORE DEADLY THAN GUNS

Exposure to a new disease is dangerous because the human body has not developed immunity. In the 16th century, European explorers travelled around the globe carrying diseases with them to which they were immune. In 1521, when Spanish explorers landed in South America, they accidentally carried smallpox with them. More Aztecs died from the disease than from Spanish guns.

➊ *This engraving shows bubonic plague victims being piled onto a wagon in the 14th century. Plague still exists today in some parts of the world, but it can usually be treated with antibiotics.*

➡ *This illustration shows the Aztecs (far right) greeting Spanish explorers. The Aztecs had no immunity to the diseases carried by their guests.*

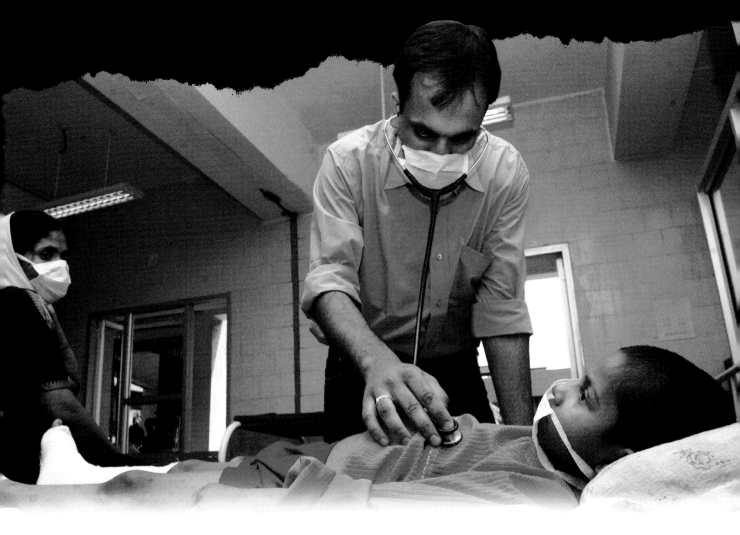

A doctor checks a child suffering from meningitis at a hospital in New Delhi, India. People in countries in the developing world face the greatest threat from disease.

GETTING THE UPPER HAND

Epidemics continued into modern times, but there were important developments. Cities in many developed countries were kept clean to reduce the chances of disease spreading, scientists developed vaccines against some of the major killers, such as smallpox, yellow fever and polio, and in the 1940s antibiotics were developed. In 1967, William S. Stewart, US Surgeon General, announced that the developed world could 'close the book on epidemic diseases'.

TODAY'S DANGERS

Despite William S. Stewart's claim, since the 1980s new diseases have been emerging, and older ones re-appearing. In 2006, scientists at a conference in the USA said new infectious diseases are emerging at a high rate and that modern living, including global travel, trade and hospitalisation, is encouraging them.

FACING THE ISSUES

Many people in developed countries believe all diseases can be cured or controlled. They have access to good medical facilities, living conditions and well-funded immunisation projects. Any outbreak of disease, such as TB, causes major concern. However, infectious diseases have never gone away from countries in the developing world. It is here that people face the greatest threat from infectious diseases – where there is little money for vaccines and medical help.

FLU EPIDEMICS

DO YOU EVER SAY: *"I've got flu", when what you've got is a bad cold? Many people do. In some ways, colds and flu are similar. Viruses cause both of them. But flu is more serious – and can be fatal.*

WHAT IS FLU?

Influenza – or flu for short – is a viral disease that attacks the respiratory system. If you get flu, you'll probably have a fever, headache, cough, sore throat and aching muscles. You may also suffer from vomiting or diarrhoea. Flu is very contagious (infectious); it spreads quickly from person to person when someone with the virus coughs or sneezes.

WINTER FLU

Flu outbreaks usually last a few weeks, but can spread through communities creating epidemics. In the USA, for example, 10–20 per cent of the population 'catch' flu every winter. Winter flu usually makes news headlines. In January 2006, several UK schools closed when thousands of school children caught flu. Many healthy people don't catch flu, but those that do usually recover well. It is the very young, elderly and sick who are most at risk. About 12,000 people die of flu every year in the UK.

⬇ *Flu vaccines help to protect people against flu. But flu viruses change constantly, so new types of vaccine have to be made every year.*

GET THE FACTS STRAIGHT

There are literally hundreds of different flu viruses. Scientists classify them into A, B, and C types. Type A viruses are found in animals, including chickens, ducks and some mammals. Types B and C are found widely in humans. Type A viruses cause scientists particular concern. They are found mainly in birds, but from time to time can 'jump species' to humans. Type A viruses are divided into subtypes according to proteins on their surface. There are two kinds of protein — haemagglutinin (H) and neuraminidase (N). The most recent type of bird flu is called H5N1.

A NEW PANDEMIC?

Pandemics occur when a new flu virus emerges, because people have no immunity to it. Based on previous evidence, scientists and medical experts fear a new flu pandemic is on its way. The virus that is worrying them is the bird flu virus, known as H5N1 (see pages 12–13).

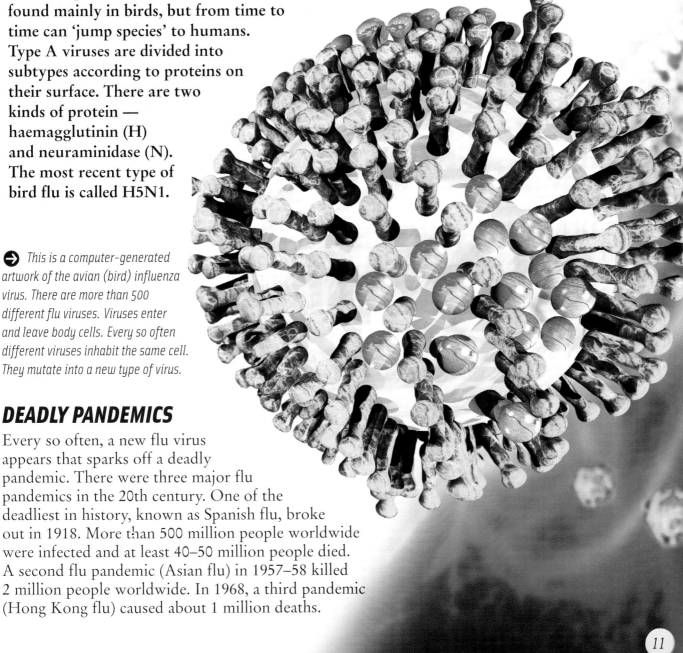

➔ *This is a computer-generated artwork of the avian (bird) influenza virus. There are more than 500 different flu viruses. Viruses enter and leave body cells. Every so often different viruses inhabit the same cell. They mutate into a new type of virus.*

DEADLY PANDEMICS

Every so often, a new flu virus appears that sparks off a deadly pandemic. There were three major flu pandemics in the 20th century. One of the deadliest in history, known as Spanish flu, broke out in 1918. More than 500 million people worldwide were infected and at least 40–50 million people died. A second flu pandemic (Asian flu) in 1957–58 killed 2 million people worldwide. In 1968, a third pandemic (Hong Kong flu) caused about 1 million deaths.

BIRD FLU

THE MEDIA WORLDWIDE *is talking about bird flu. Experts warn that it may lead to the next major flu pandemic. But what is bird flu? What are the risks to humans? Will it be as bad as some people think?*

WHAT IS BIRD FLU?

Avian influenza – popularly known as bird flu – is a type of flu that affects birds. The virus lives in the guts of wild and domestic birds, such as chickens, geese, ducks and swans. It usually causes little harm, but sometimes it makes birds sick and kills them.

⬇ *Masked and gowned workers clear away dead birds that have been infected with bird flu in Malaysia. Many birds are being culled to prevent the spread of bird flu.*

BIRD SICKNESS EPIDEMIC

In 1997, chickens in Hong Kong began dying from a bird flu virus. Scientists identified the virus as H5N1. It died away but re-emerged in 2003 and since then millions of birds have developed bird flu. It is the biggest epidemic of bird flu ever recorded, affecting birds in Asia, Africa, Europe, and the Middle East. In 2006, a dead swan in Scotland was found to be carrying the H5N1 virus.

CAN HUMANS GET BIRD FLU?

Evidence shows that virus H5N1 can 'jump species' from birds to humans. As of April 2006, there had been 194 reported cases of bird flu in humans, mostly in Southeast Asia, but also Turkey, Iraq, Azerbaijan and Egypt. By the summer of 2006, 109 people had died. Close contact with diseased birds on farms seemed to be the main source of infection.

FACING THE ISSUES

The World Health Organization estimates that 2–7.5 million people might die and millions more could be infected if bird flu mutates and spreads easily from person-to-person. Governments around the world are taking steps to reduce the chances of this happening. In Denmark, after cases of H5N1 were confirmed in May 2006, the authorities culled nearby farm birds and set up bird flu surveillance zones. As a precaution anti-viral drugs and handwashes were also distributed to people living in the area.

WILL THERE BE A PANDEMIC?

No one knows if bird flu will lead to a human flu pandemic. So far, there is no hard evidence that humans who contract bird flu can infect other humans, but it was reported that a Thai woman died of bird flu after nursing her sick daughter. However, this was an isolated case and the disease did not spread into the community.

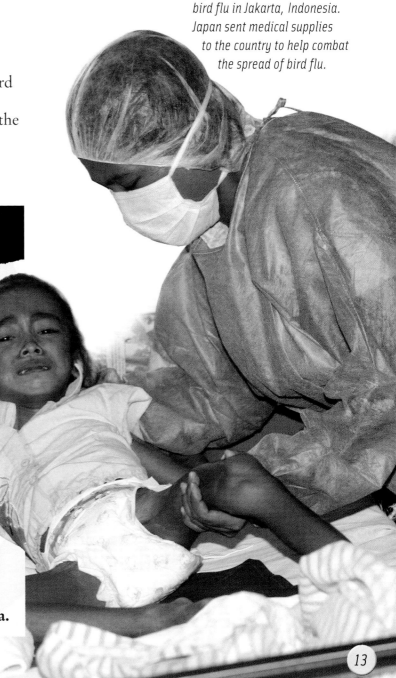

A young girl suffering from bird flu in Jakarta, Indonesia. Japan sent medical supplies to the country to help combat the spread of bird flu.

EBOLA FEVER

IN THE MID-1970s, doctors in Africa faced a new and deadly disease. It was called Ebola fever, after the Ebola River in Central Africa. It is one of a group of haemorrhagic fevers, so called because they cause severe bleeding, or haemorrhaging. When Ebola fever first broke out, it made headline news. Books and films also used it as a theme because its symptoms are so terrible.

⬆ *A hospital in Uganda during the Ebola epidemic. The hospital was quarantined to deal with people suffering from Ebola.*

EBOLA OUTBREAKS

Doctors first identified Ebola fever in 1976, when outbreaks occurred in Sudan and what was then Zaire. People developed a high fever, and within a few days many died from organ failure and severe bleeding. Since then, there have been Ebola epidemics in Sudan, Gabon, the Democratic Republic of Congo, Uganda, and the Ivory Coast. Hundreds of people have died, including health workers and doctors.

A DEADLY VIRUS

Ebola is one of the deadliest viruses known. It probably lives in non-human primates – monkeys and chimpanzees – who can also develop Ebola fever. Humans become infected through close contact with primates or eating infected meat. The disease moves quickly, spread by contact with body fluids including infected blood and vomit. It kills 50–90 per cent of those who contract the disease.

FACING THE ISSUES

Ebola, like many diseases in Africa, is made worse by poverty. Hospitals are poorly equipped, hypodermic needles are re-used (which spreads infection), and health workers are put at risk because masks and protective gowns are in short supply. Friends and relatives who help with nursing can also spread the disease through a community. Even burial customs, which involve people touching and preparing the dead, carry health risks so are now discouraged.

A DIFFICULT FIGHT

Treating and containing a disease like Ebola in Africa is difficult. Hospitals, doctors and medical equipment are limited. When Ebola broke out in Uganda, the United Nations (UN), WHO and American Center for Disease Prevention and Control sent medical teams, researchers and equipment. There were also appeals for international aid. Villages were quarantined to try to stop the disease spreading.

HOW FAR WILL EBOLA SPREAD?

Ebola is highly infectious. War, poverty and the movement of soldiers and refugees have helped to spread the disease through Central and Western Africa. In 2001, WHO announced that Uganda was virtually Ebola free, but epidemics have continued elsewhere in Africa. Experts fear that with the growth of tourism in Africa, the virus is only an aeroplane flight away. They fear one day Ebola could move from Africa to another continent.

⬇ Scientists testing the body of a monkey suspected of carrying the Ebola virus. WHO funds research into diseases so that scientists can help to wipe them out.

15

HIV/AIDS IS TODAY'S NUMBER ONE

deadly pandemic. Since 1981, more than 28 million people worldwide have died of Aids. Over 40 million people are infected. Many are children and young people, and more than half are women.

GET THE FACTS STRAIGHT

UNAIDS (the Joint United Nations Programme on HIV/Aids) produces regular information and statistics about HIV/Aids. According to recent figures:

- 40.3 million people are living with HIV/Aids. Of these, 2 million are children;

- young people (aged 15–24) account for half of all new HIV infections worldwide. More than 6,000 become infected with HIV every day;

- nearly 60 per cent of all people with HIV/Aids live in sub-Saharan Africa. More than 20 per cent live in Asia. About 5 per cent live in developed countries;

- 12 million children in Africa are orphans because their parents have died of Aids.

A MYSTERIOUS DISEASE

Aids first appeared in 1981, when doctors in the USA saw unusual symptoms among homosexual men. Some drug addicts and people who had received blood transfusions also displayed these symptoms, including skin cancers, weight loss and unexplained tiredness. Infected people eventually died. Cases appeared in Africa, too.

A NEW VIRUS

In 1983 epidemiologists (people who study epidemics) identified the virus causing Aids. It was HIV or human immunodeficiency virus. HIV is a particular type of virus, called a retrovirus, that attacks the immune system, taking over white blood cells and making it impossible for the body to fight disease. Once white blood cells decrease to a critical point, a person is said to have Aids – acquired immune deficiency syndrome. Infection passes through blood, sexual fluids and breast milk.

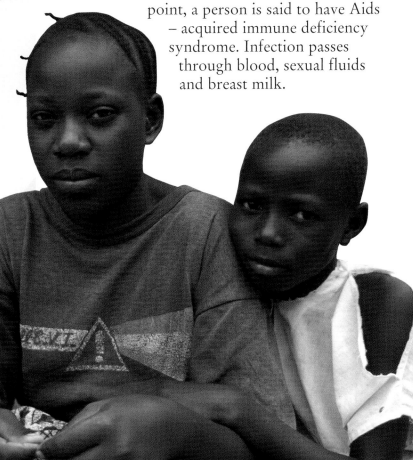

◀ HIV/Aids is destroying families across the whole
of central and southern Africa. These children have
lost their mother and father. Women catch HIV from
unprotected sex and pass the virus to unborn children,
and to children through breast-feeding.

⬆ A massive quilt records the names of those who
have died of Aids. Public displays help to overcome
prejudices and raise public awareness. Health
promotion and education programmes help to prevent
new cases.

HIV/AIDS PANDEMIC

Since it emerged in 1981, HIV/Aids
has spread rapidly throughout the world.
In central and southern Africa, Aids is
wiping out a whole generation, and numbers
of infected people are rising in India, China
and Eastern Europe. There is no cure,
although anti-viral drugs have been
developed that slow the progress of the
disease. These are widely available in the
world's developed countries, but developing
countries cannot always afford them.

POLITICAL AND SOCIAL BARRIERS

Aids cannot be cured, but it can be prevented
with better education and treated with drugs.
Governments and international health agencies
work together to tackle the disease (see page
25). In 1996, the UN set up UNAIDS, a joint
programme to help overcome prejudices which
arise because Aids is seen as a sexual disease. In
the 1980s, Aids was one of the world's biggest
news stories. Today, the problem is far greater
but it receives less media coverage because it is
largely under control in developed countries.

SARS

IN FEBRUARY 2003, *reports appeared of a new flu-like disease spreading across Southeast Asia. It had also appeared in Canada. By April 2003, it had spread to 29 countries and WHO had issued a global alert. The disease was known as SARS.*

WHAT IS SARS?

SARS is short for Severe Acute Respiratory Syndrome. It affects breathing and, if not treated quickly, can be fatal. SARS is caused by a virus and is transmitted by infected mucus in coughs and sneezes. Someone with SARS can take up to 10 days to become ill.

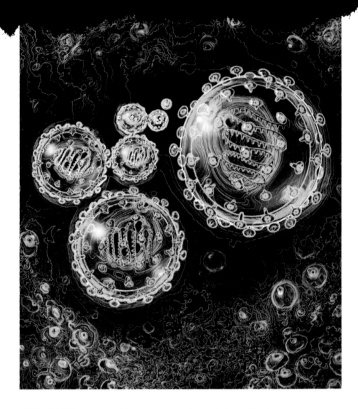

⬆ *SARS is caused by a coronavirus. It has distinctive crown shaped halo, which gives the virus its name.*

⬅ *Some people in China wearing face masks. They hope to reduce the chances of catching SARS.*

WHERE AND WHEN DID SARS BEGIN?

SARS began in Guangdong Province, southern China in November 2002. People fell ill with flu-like symptoms that developed into life-threatening pneumonia. The Chinese government kept the outbreak secret because they feared panic and loss of trade from tourism. In February 2003, a Chinese professor of respiratory medicine, who had become infected, travelled to Hong Kong where he died. SARS spread throughout Hong Kong, and finally became public knowledge.

INVESTIGATING A GLOBAL ALERT

SARS spread rapidly, mainly in China and Hong Kong, and to Taiwan, Singapore and Canada. Thousands of people were infected in China, and hundreds of people died. WHO declared the new virus "a worldwide health threat" and co-ordinated laboratory teams in 10 different countries to uncover the cause. Eventually, experts announced that SARS was caused by a previously unknown coronavirus. It lives in civet cats and racoons, which are traditionally used in Chinese medicine. The virus had mutated and jumped species to infect humans.

⬇ *Travellers returning from countries where SARS existed were screened at airports by special heat-detecting cameras. One of the first symptoms of SARS was a rise in body temperature.*

END OF AN EPIDEMIC

Isolating patients and strict precautionary health measures helped to contain the epidemic. In July 2003, WHO announced that the SARS epidemic was under control. Even so, more than 8,000 people had been infected, of whom nearly 1,000 died. Since then, there have been four small but easily contained outbreaks.

FACING THE ISSUES

SARS shows how quickly an outbreak can become an epidemic today. It only took days for SARS to be spread around the world by infected people travelling by air. One traveller flew from Hong Kong to Frankfurt and Munich in Germany, onto London, back to Germany and then to Hong Kong, without even knowing he had the disease. SARS also demonstrates the need for government honesty. When SARS hit the news in February 2003, it had already existed in China for several months.

FOOD FEARS

MOST PEOPLE IN THE DEVELOPED
world eat well and fairly cheaply.
Convenience and so-called 'junk'
foods are very popular. But
cheap food comes at a
price. Intensive farming
methods and modern food
production bring their
own dangers. Every so
often, news headlines
warn that our food can
cause deadly diseases.

 Cows infected with BSE were destroyed. New, tighter
controls were introduced by the UK government to prevent
the disease becoming more widespread.

MYSTERY BRAIN DISEASE

In the mid-1980s, some cows in
the UK developed disturbing
symptoms. They staggered, behaved
aggressively and started dying. Autopsies
revealed that sick cows had brains riddled
with tiny sponge-like holes. The disease
was diagnosed as Bovine Spongiform
Encephalopathy (BSE), an infectious
disease that causes fatal damage to the
nervous system. The media
nicknamed it 'Mad Cow Disease'.

WHAT CAUSED IT?

Research showed that BSE belonged to the
same family of brain wasting diseases as scrapie,
a disease found in sheep. It turned out that
farmers were feeding cattle with meat and bone
meal produced from offal – brain, spinal cord,
intestines and other organs – rendered down
from sheep.

CHEAP FEED

It seems strange that farmers fed meat products
to cows, which usually eat only grass. But the
feed was rich in protein, which helped the cows
to grow. It was also cheap to produce, which
helped profits. In 1988, the UK government
banned the use of sheep offal in cattle feed and
cattle suspected of having BSE were destroyed.

HUMANS AND BSE

The European Union banned the sale of beef from the UK, even though the UK government insisted that humans were not at risk from BSE. But by 1996, ten young people had died from a new type of a rare brain-wasting disease called Creutzfeld-Jakob Disease (CJD). It was confirmed that this new variant CJD could be caught from BSE infected beef. About 150 people have died from vCJD, but it takes a long time to develop. Experts fear more people may die from vCJD. The European ban on UK beef ended in 2006.

➡ *Arnaud Eboli was the third person to die as a result of vCJD in France, 2001.*

GET THE FACTS STRAIGHT

Most types of food can become harmful if they are contaminated. Food poisoning occurs when you eat undercooked meats, or dairy products, such as mayonnaise, that are left exposed to harmful bacteria. It may affect only one person, or cause an epidemic. Bacteria that cause food poisoning include e. coli, salmonella and listeria. Antibiotics are used to treat food poisoning. Farmers also use antibiotics to treat diseases in cattle, so they enter the food chain. Unfortunately, some bacteria, including e. coli, can then become resistant to the antibiotics used to treat human illnesses.

⬅ *Hamburgers are a favourite food for many young people. Poor food processing can cause contamination and food poisoning. Health inspectors check fast-food outlets and restaurants to make sure they are kept clean.*

MOSQUITOES AND EPIDEMICS

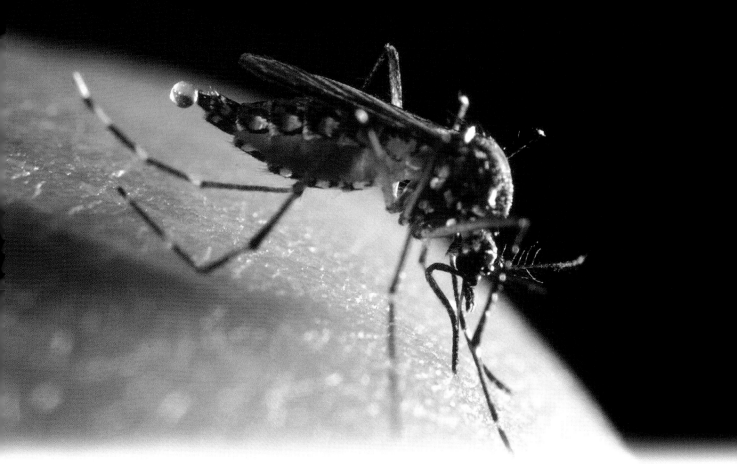

CLIMATE CHANGE, TOGETHER with human behaviour, encourages the spread of infectious diseases. Scientists tell us we are in a period of global warming, with rising air temperatures, and more droughts, flooding and hurricanes. These natural disasters provide perfect conditions for disease-carrying organisms and the animals or insects that transport them.

⬆ Mosquitoes carry yellow fever, malaria and dengue fever. When they suck human blood, they deposit saliva, which contains disease-causing parasites.

MALARIA

One disease-carrying insect is the mosquito, which lives in warm, humid conditions. Its bite transfers tiny disease-causing parasites, including one that causes malaria, a deadly infectious disease. Malaria was thought to be under control, but it still kills about 1 million people a year. Most of these are children in Africa.

WEST NILE FEVER

Diseases carried by mosquitoes, once known only in Africa, are now breaking out elsewhere. In 1999, West Nile fever, an infectious disease that can lead to serious illnesses such as meningitis, broke out near New York City, killing nine people. In 2003, nearly 10,000 cases were reported in the USA, including 264 deaths. There have been outbreaks in parts of Europe, Australia and Israel.

DENGUE FEVER

Another disease carried by mosquitoes is dengue fever, a severe but usually non-fatal illness. It has existed in Africa, South America and Southeast Asia for many years. In 2002, the first ever case was reported in Maui, Hawaii. Dengue fever hit the headlines in 2004 when an epidemic in Indonesia affected over 58,000 people, killing more than 650 of them. Stagnant water from heavy rain was thought to have led to a mosquito population explosion.

NATURAL DISASTERS

Most mosquito-related diseases are usually associated with Africa, where poverty, war, famine and extreme climate conditions encourage their spread. But natural disasters, such as the Indonesian tsunami in 2004, which can't be controlled also encourage their spread. Even in developed countries a population can be put at risk, such as during the floods in New Orleans, USA, which followed Hurricane Katrina in 2005.

➡ *Stagnant water provides a perfect breeding ground for mosquitoes.*

FACING THE ISSUES

One of the problems with malaria and other diseases carried by mosquitoes is that measures once used to control them are now less effective. Some mosquitoes have developed resistance to pesticides. The parasites that cause malaria are also developing resistance to drugs, such as chloroquine, commonly used to treat the disease. Health agencies concentrate on preventative measures, including mosquito nets, which are very effective, and cleaning areas of water where mosquitoes breed.

PREVENTING EPIDEMICS

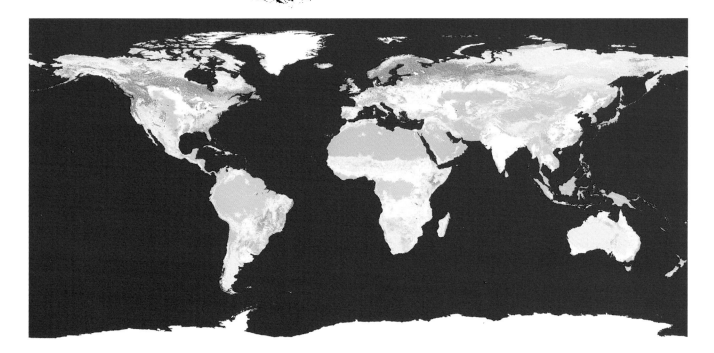

EPIDEMICS HAVE occurred constantly throughout human history and are not likely to go away. Today, we are facing new diseases as well as trying to cope with changing disease patterns. But there are positive developments. Advances in technology can help us to predict when and where an epidemic may occur. Governments and health agencies can then introduce measures to prevent an outbreak becoming an epidemic.

SATELLITE MONITORING

The outbreak of some diseases, such as malaria and yellow fever, is affected by changes in the weather. Heavy rains or flooding encourage mosquitoes to breed. Epidemiologists use weather satellites to track weather conditions, and predict the possibility of an outbreak of diseases carried by mosquitoes.

INFORMATION HIGHWAY

Diseases travel fast but so too does electronic information. Preventing epidemics involves surveillance, monitoring, and information gathering and exchange. All this can happen on the Internet. There are many websites today where information about new diseases or potential epidemics is posted.

⬆ *A computer-generated satellite map like this can be used to plot global weather patterns. By knowing about changes in the weather, scientists may be able to predict outbreaks of insect-borne diseases such as yellow fever.*

➡ *Children are often most at risk from infectious diseases. This International Committee of the Red Cross worker in El Salvador is teaching children about basic disease prevention.*

FACING THE ISSUES

International co-operation is essential to try and combat some major diseases, such as malaria and HIV/Aids. In 1998, WHO together with the United Nations International Children's Emergency Fund (UNICEF), the World Bank and other agencies formed the Roll Back Malaria partnership. Its aim is to halve malaria cases by 2010. The UN and other agencies have also combined to combat HIV/Aids worldwide. Health promotion and education, effective funding, accurate monitoring, and the involvement of local authorities all play a major part in preventing epidemics.

GLOBAL EXCHANGE

Some websites operate as unofficial 'early warning' systems. They include the Global Public Health Intelligence Network (GPHIN), which was developed by the Public Health Agency of Canada, and Pro-MED mail (the Program for Monitoring Emerging Diseases). Organisations and individuals worldwide not only post information about emerging diseases or outbreaks of disease, but also track the progress of a disease.

OFFICIAL SURVEILLANCE

The World Health Organization (WHO) was set up in 1948 by the UN. Its job is to combat diseases worldwide. The work of WHO involves surveillance, tracking and monitoring the progress of epidemics and advising governments on how to combat epidemics. It has set up a 'network of networks' that links local, regional, national and international networks of laboratories and medical centres to form a global surveillance network. Other important agencies include the US Center for Disease Control and Prevention.

THE WAY GOVERNMENTS deal with epidemics varies depending on which part of the world they are in. All governments want to protect the health of their citizens. How well they actually do that, and the measures they use, depends on their financial resources and health services.

Government co-operation and sufficient resources can help to overcome most epidemics. For example, smallpox, one of the oldest diseases known to exist, is highly infectious and has killed millions of people worldwide. A vaccine was developed in the 18th century. By 1900, through mass vaccination, smallpox had been almost completely wiped out in the USA and Europe. However, it remained a killer in developing countries. In 1967, WHO formed the Global Commission for the Eradication of Smallpox. The aim was to contain every new outbreak and vaccinate everyone who came into contact with the infection. In 1980, WHO announced that smallpox had been eradicated worldwide.

CLOSING BORDERS

Developed countries are free from most deadly infectious diseases, such as cholera or typhoid. Their governments do not want these diseases re-emerging. People who travel to these countries from places where diseases are endemic must prove they have been vaccinated against them. Sometimes, when an epidemic breaks out, the government stops people entering the country, although this rarely prevents a disease from spreading.

⬆ When bird flu arrived in Turkey, the government introduced border controls to prevent anyone from bringing in infected birds.

INTERNATIONAL AID

Developed countries have enough money to finance their own health services and projects. But governments in less developed countries do not always have the resources to fight epidemics in this way. International aid from charities, agencies and wealthier nations can help. But other conditions that encourage disease, including war, famine, and poor sanitation and health services also need to be tackled to reduce the chances of an epidemic occurring.

⊘ *Mothers wait to have their children immunised against polio in Nigeria. Large-scale immunisation projects need to continue if some epidemics are to be prevented in future.*

VACCINATION AND MASS IMMUNISATION

Vaccines are the first line of defence against infectious diseases. In developed countries, vaccinating children has helped to control measles and whooping cough. However, not all countries can afford to do this. When an epidemic breaks out, international agencies, such as the International Committee of the Red Cross or Medecins sans Frontières, carry out mass immunisation programmes.

PLANNING AND INFORMATION

Governments draw up emergency plans for possible epidemics. Recent outbreaks of bird flu across Europe have led some governments to put these into place. They check hospital resources and maintain stockpiles of drugs and vaccines. They also set up surveillance zones if a disease breaks out, distribute information and set up help telephone lines for the public.

WHAT CAN YOU DO?

YOU MAY NOT be able to stop an epidemic, but there is a lot you can do to promote health and contribute to the fight against disease. You can keep informed about hygiene and food production. You can stay healthy yourself and help to keep others healthy around you. You can also keep yourself informed about the state of the world's health.

WHAT DO YOU THINK?

⬆ *Always make sure your food, especially meat, is cooked properly to kill any harmful bacteria (see page 21).*

This book has given you some information about epidemics. Now what do you think:

- How could humans cause epidemics?
- Do you think people should travel less?
- Why might stricter laws about food hygiene and production reduce the chances of an epidemic occurring?
- How could governments help to keep us healthy?
- What could governments in developed countries do to help developing countries fight disease?
- How can epidemics end when so many people live in poverty around the world?

STAYING HEALTHY

The best way to avoid getting sick is to keep yourself healthy. This means taking plenty of exercise and eating a healthy, well-balanced diet. Try to avoid eating too many junk foods and sugary meals and drinks. Instead, include plenty of water, fresh fruit and vegetables in your daily diet. Make sure meat and fish are stored and cooked properly.

DO NOT INFECT OTHERS

Epidemics happen when germs spread from person to person. If you become ill with a cold, flu or other infectious disease, do not pass it on to others. A sneeze travels at about 160 kilometres per hour, and is full of germs. Put your hand in front of your mouth and nose when you sneeze or cough. Use paper tissues and throw them away. If you are really ill you should see your doctor. He or she may suggest that you stay away from school for a couple of days, until you are no longer infectious. Your doctor may also prescribe you some medicine, such as antibiotics.

BE HYGIENIC

Germs breed in dirty places, so help to keep things clean and hygienic. Don't forget, you can't actually see germs, but they are there. Wash your hands with soap and warm water after going to the bathroom, and before eating. Make sure kitchen surfaces are always clean. Cover food or store it in the fridge, and do not put uncooked meat near other foods. Rubbish, such as empty cans and scraps of food can attract disease-carrying insects. Wash out and recycle cans, and put food scraps and packaging into a sealed bin.

➡ *As the rhyme says 'coughs and sneezes spread diseases', so cover your nose and mouth to reduce the chances of spreading germs.*

STAY INFORMED

There is a lot of information about epidemics in the news and on the Internet. Make sure you use good sources (see page 31). Find out more about epidemics, and see if there is anything you can do. Perhaps you and your friends could raise money for a children's health charity, or debate the subject of epidemics in your class at school. There may be something you can do locally, such as clearing a dirty pond.

GLOSSARY

Aids A disease of the immune system, which destroys certain white blood cells. Stands for aquired immune deficiency syndrome.

Antibiotic A substance that kills or weakens harmful bacteria in the body.

Antibody A substance produced by the immune system that identifies and fights harmful bacteria and viruses which invade the body. Once antibodies have overcome disease, the body remains immune to that particular disease.

Autopsy Medical examination of a dead body to find out the cause of death.

Bacteria Microscopic living organisms. Bacteria live all around us, and in our bodies. Many are harmless; some cause disease.

Center for Disease Control and Prevention (CDC) The main US government agency that deals with epidemics in the USA and worldwide.

Contagious Infectious.

Cull To collect animals together and kill them as a precaution against the spread of disease.

Endemic Used to describe a disease that occurs in one particular region only.

Epidemic Describes a disease that spreads from its place of origin to affect many people.

Eradicate To destroy or get rid of something so that it does not come back.

Germ A micro-organism that causes disease.

HIV Short for human immunodeficiency virus – the virus that causes Aids.

Immune system The body's own defence system. It fights incoming infectious diseases.

Mutate To change from one thing into another.

Outbreak When a disease suddenly breaks out. It may lead to an epidemic.

Pandemic A global or widespread epidemic that affects many countries throughout the world.

Protein A type of chemical found in most organisms.

Quarantine Isolating people or animals that may have been exposed to an infectious disease.

Respiratory system The body system, including the lungs, that breathes in oxygen and breathes out carbon dioxide.

Stagnant Describes water that does not flow, leading to a build up of bacteria and other organisms.

Tuberculosis (TB) A disease caused by bacteria that affects the lungs. It can be fatal.

Vaccine A substance that contains weakened or dead microbes that cause a particular disease. Doctors vaccinate people to protect them against that particular disease. It works by stimulating the body's immune system to produce antibodies.

vCJD New variant CJD (Creutzfeldt-Jakob disease).

Virus A 'package' of tiny chemical particles that invades living cells and can cause disease. Viruses cannot be seen with the human eye, except through a powerful microscope.

World Health Organization (WHO) An agency founded by the United Nations (UN) in 1948 to advise countries about health care. It also tracks and attempts to control epidemics worldwide and provides information about epidemics.

FURTHER INFORMATION

Find out more about epidemics on these websites. Most have weblinks to take you to other useful sites.

World Health Organization (WHO)

The WHO is part of the United Nations (UN). It is concerned with global health. Its site includes all sorts of information about health and sickness around the world. It has information on individual diseases, and health projects.
http://www.who.int/en

Center for Disease Control and Prevention (CDC)

Agency of the US Department of Health and Human Services. The CDC is mainly concerned with disease prevention and control in the United States but CDC works globally as well. The website is a very good source of information about all today's epidemics and infectious diseases. They also have sites designed specifically for children and young people.
http://www.bt.cdc.gov

BAM! Body and Mind

A website created by the CDC for young people aged 9–13 years old. Contains lots of information about illnesses and healthy lifestyles. Also includes quizzes and plenty of fun activities.
http://www.bam.gov/index.htm

European Centre for Disease Prevention and Control (ECDC)

European Union (EU) agency that has been created to help strengthen Europe's defences against infectious diseases such as influenza, SARS and HIV/Aids.
http://www.ecdc.eu.int

Health Protection Agency (HPA)

Set up in 2005, the HPA co-ordinates work on protecting public health in the UK.
http://www.hpa.org.uk/hpa/default.htm

BBC websites

You can use the BBC news website for up-to-date news about health issues around the world. Just enter the name of the disease or epidemic in the search box. Alternatively, you can browse through the BBC health site for information on all aspects of health.
http://news.bbc.co.uk
http://www.bbc.co.uk/health

Communicable Diseases Network Australia (CDNA)

Set up in 1989 to provide information on all infectious diseases. Part of the Australian Government's Department of Health and Ageing.
http://www.health.gov.au/internet/wcms/Publishing.nsf/Content/cda-cdna-index.htm

Think Quest: Anatomy of an Epidemic

An interactive website that looks at what epidemics are, what causes them and how they can be prevented. Contains maps and quizzes.
http://library.thinkquest.org/11170

Virtual Information Centre

This is an online resource that gives you the latest information about infectious diseases. It describes diseases, symptoms, treatments and the latest developments.
http://www.virtualinfectioncentre.com

Danish Ministry of the Interior and Health

This website from the government of Denmark can be viewed in English. Click on 'health' for up-to-date news and information about staying healthy and the Danish health care system.
http://www.im.dk

INDEX